The Development of Psycho-Analysis

Classics in Psychoanalysis

Edited by
George H. Pollock, M.D., Ph.D.
Chicago Institute for Psychoanalysis

Monograph 4

The Development of Psycho-Analysis

Dr. S. Ferenczi *(Budapest)*

Dr. Otto Rank *(Vienna)*

AUTHORIZED ENGLISH
By
CAROLINE NEWTON
MEMBER OF THE
VIENNA PSYCHO–ANALYTICAL SOCIETY

INTERNATIONAL UNIVERSITIES PRESS, INC.
Madison   Connecticut

Library of Congress Cataloging-in-Publication Data

Ferenczi, Sandor, 1873-1933.
    The development of psychoanalysis.

    (Classics in psychoanalysis; monograph 4)
    Reprint. Originally published: New York:
Nervous and Mental Disease Pub. Co., 1925
    Translation of: Entwicklungsziele der Psychoanalyse.
    Includes bibliographies and index.
    1. Psychoanalysis. I. Rank, Otto, 1884-1939.
II. Title. III. Series: Classics in psychoanalysis;
monograph no. 4. [DNLM: 1. Psychoanalytic Theory.
2. Psychoanalytic Therapy. W1 CL122D no. 4 /
Wm 460.6 F349e 1925a]
RC504.F3813   1986   150.19'5   86-7198
ISBN 0-8236-1197-3

Manufactured in the United States of America.

CONTENTS.

FOREWORD

It is valuable to occasionally study the history and development of a discipline—especially of one that is constantly involved in studying the past of an individual. As the translator notes, this monographic statement was written sixty-three years ago. Drs. Ferenczi and Rank, early pioneers in psychoanalysis, later departed in various ways from the more traditional approaches of psychoanalysis. Today when we observe such departures, extensions, modifications of our theories and techniques, it is useful to go back in time and read of earlier workers who were involved in modifications. Unfortunately such individuals in the past and present do not have their ideas seriously evaluated according to the canons of clinical and scientific assessment. Instead they may be labeled as deviationists, deviants, or even worse and political and personal attacks can ensue. We have seen how this was used against Freud in the past and even today his detractors resort to *ad hominem* accusations instead of assessing his ideas for their utility, their germinative stimulation of new ideas, and their value in understanding man.

The authors' essay can be seen as an historic report of what they saw as a developmental "state of the art" of psychoanalysis in 1922. Some of their arguments and grapplings are still current, e.g., is psychoanalysis a science or an art? Some of their assertions and statements seemingly have less or little validity today. Some are still very current six decades after publication.

The current arguments and questions about Freud, his ideas, and even about psychoanalysis itself have a familiar ring to them. We do know that Freud himself regarded psychoanalysis as a number of connected but distinct theories, e.g., how the mind functions, the development of the personality, the meaning of dreams and slips, the

vii

significance of social, religious, and cultural factors on internal practices, and the applications of psychoanalytic findings to therapy. From this sprang ideas about technique and psychopathology and such fundamental concepts as, for example, transference, repetition compulsion, meaning of symptoms. The current debates on how and if psychoanalytic treatment cures opens up new areas for discussion. Freud's main interest was in the dynamic unconscious; the clinical situation was to be the source of data for his and other analysts' theories. The idea of treatment in some ways was of lesser importance. This is obviously not what patients hoped for and we know that insight, identification, working through, catharsis—all components of analytic therapy—are of great benefit to suitable patients, but whether this is cure or rehabilitation or newer adaptations without fundamental conflict removal requires more research of the therapeutic process, outcome, and follow-up studies.

If one views psychoanalysis as a "humane discipline" and not a "natural science," the arguments of current philosophers of science may be less significant than if one holds the contrary point of view. Ferenczi and Rank were caught in this dilemma and decades after their volume was written we still are unclear about this issue. One can use reality testing—my description of scientific method— without having to address the question of whether psychoanalysis is or is not a natural science. Freud derived his insights from himself, his patients, the great philosophers, playwrights, poets, and artists; he sought to understand the human experience. But Freud was also a physician and a researcher, and he earned his living as a clinician. These roles also played a part in the development of his theories and influenced his students' contributions. He was also a magnificent writer and won the Goethe Prize for his great literary talent.

This volume is an historic one. It should be read keeping this in mind. It also relates to technique as Ferenczi and Rank viewed this in the therapeutic process. It does, however, have relevance to ideas of today—transference and repetition, displacement, resistance, interpretation, fixation, etc. Some will object to the use of "old terminology" or "ancient concepts," but careful reading can be fruitful if one bears in mind when this monograph was written and how much of it may still be useful today.

The authors write "in every correct analysis the analyst plays all possible roles for the unconscious of the patient; it only depends upon him always to recognize this at the proper time and under certain circumstances to consciously make use of it. Particularly important is the role of the two parental images—father and mother—in which the analyst actually constantly alternates (transference and resistance)" (p. 41). This simple statement has much validity today and describes directly what others have subsequently elaborated upon in great detail. Ferenczi and Rank also write in a meaningful way about "a kind of narcissistic counter transference" (p. 41) in the analyst indicating an awareness of ideas that are currently being explored in depth. It is our belief that the readers of this brief monograph can learn more than history from it and hence we are again making it available by reprinting it.

George H. Pollock, M.D., Ph.D.
President
Institute for Psychoanalysis of Chicago

February, 1985

TRANSLATOR'S PREFACE.

The translator of this slender volume had the good fortune to be studying psycho-analysis in Vienna at the time of its first appearance in German in December, 1923. Dr. Rank and Dr. Ferenczi are admittedly Professor Freud's most brilliant and original followers, but the "Entwicklungsziele der Psychoanalyse" attracted a quite special attention. Both men, in addition to their other great contributions to psycho-analysis, are particularly skilful therapeutists and this book offers an opportunity for practicing analysts to see the development of analytic technique and the special angles of two of its most successful practitioners.

The book was written in the summer of 1922, somewhat modified and altered by the events of the International Psycho-analytical Congress, held in Berlin in September of that year, and completed in 1923. The authors apologize for some of the deficiencies of structure on account of this history of its origin.

The critical part of the work was originally written by Dr. Ferenczi, the didactic chapter "The Analytical Situation" by Dr. Rank and the work then jointly revised. As will be seen from the above, the book is intended primarily for practicing analysts and will appeal only to serious students of psycho-analysis. Although the number of its readers will therefore be limited it seems important to offer an English version for those adherents of the science who are not familiar with the German language, but who nevertheless wish to keep up with the recent development of analytic technique.

CAROLINE NEWTON.

DAYLESFORD, PENNA.

August, 1924.

CHAPTER I.

Psycho-analysis has developed, as is well known, in the course of almost thirty years, from a simple medical method of treatment of certain neurotic disturbances to an extensive scientific theoretic system which is slowly but steadily growing and seems to lead to a new interpretation of life.

To follow the development of this process step by step, and to study, on the one hand the reciprocal relation of the therapeutic method and the medical technique, and on the other the scientific development in detail, would mean nothing less than writing a continuation of "The History of the Psycho-Analytic Movement."[1] By attacking this problem which cannot as yet be solved, it would be unavoidable to touch upon questions which extend greatly beyond the subject of psycho-analysis as such. One would have to consider the relationship between the facts dealt with by a science and this science itself. Such a task is in itself extremely difficult, because it leads to a discussion of the fundamental principles of our whole scientific method, but it becomes almost impossible in the case of psycho-analysis, which is still in a stage of development. And we who are active participants in the process, who are representatives of both the medical-therapeutic, as well as the scientific-theoretic group find it very difficult to make an objective estimate of the facts about these inter-relations.

[1] See Freud "Zur Geschichte der psychoanalytischen Bewegung (Sammlung kleiner Schriften zur Neurosenlehre 4. Folge). English Translation this Series No. 25.

On the other hand one cannot deny that in the last ten years, a state of increasing confusion, particularly in respect to the practical problems, has been gaining ground among psycho-analysts. In contrast to the rapid growth of the psycho-analytical theory, the technical and therapeutic factor which was originally the heart of the matter and the actual stimulus to every important advance in the theory has been strikingly neglected, in the literature, as well as in practice. This could give the false impression [1a] that the development of the technique had stood still in the meantime, particularly since Freud himself has always been, as is well known, extremely reserved on this point, to such an extent, indeed, that it is almost ten years since he has published any work on the subject. His few technical articles, which are collected in the "Sammlung kleiner Schriften zur Neurosenlehre" IV. Serie—were, for analysts who had not themselves undergone an analysis, the only correct indication for their technical activity although they, according to Freud's point of view, are certainly incomplete and in certain points, on account of the present development, antiquated and seem to need modification. One can therefore understand why the majority of those analysts, who were dependent upon the study of the literature, adhered too rigidly to these technical rules, and could not find the connection to the stages of progress which the science of analysis had made in the meantime.

We were dissatisfied with this state of affairs and found

[1a] The work of Ferenczi to establish active intervention in the technique constitutes an exception. These attempts were either ignored or incorrectly interpreted by the majority of analysts, perhaps because the author, at that time in emphasizing the new interpretation, did not sufficiently make clear to the reader how this point of view fits into the hitherto prevailing theory and technique. (See "Weiterer Ausbau der aktiven Technik in der Psychoanalyse" Zeitschrift VII, 1922.)

ourselves repeatedly forced to pause in our practical work in order to take account of these difficulties and problems. In doing this we found that our technical ability had made important strides in the meantime, the completely conscious comprehension and value of which placed us in a position to perceptibly increase our knowledge. We finally found it necessary, in the face of an evident and general need for a clarification of the situation, to inform others of our experiences, and we think that we shall do this best, by first attempting to describe in what way we practice psycho-analysis to-day, and what we now mean by it. Only then will it be possible for us to understand the difficulties which appear on all sides and how we hope to remedy them.

In order to do this we must connect directly with Freud's last technical work ("Remembering, Repeating and Working through," 1914) in which a different degree of importance is attached to the three factors mentioned in the title, inasmuch as remembering is treated as the actual aim of psycho-analytic work, whereas the desire to repeat instead of remembering, is regarded as a symptom of resistance and is therefore recommended to be avoided. From the standpoint of the compulsion to repeat, it is, however, not only absolutely unavoidable, that the patient should, during the cure, repeat a large part of his process of development, but also as experience has shown, it is a matter of just those portions which cannot be really experienced from memory, so that there is no other way open to the patient than that of repeating, as well as no other means for the analyst to seize the essential unconscious material. It is now a question of understanding also this form of communication, the so-called language of gesture, as Ferenczi has called it, and of explaining it to the patient. The neurotic symptoms, indeed, as Freud has taught us, are themselves simply distorted forms of expression of the unconscious which at first are not understood.

The first practical necessity resulting from this insight was not only not to suppress the tendency to repetition in the analysis,[2] but even to require it, provided, of course, that one knows how to master it, for otherwise the most important material cannot be expressed and dealt with. On the other hand, certain resistances—perhaps even biologically founded ones—oppose themselves to the repetition compulsion, particularly the feeling of anxiety and of guilt which we can only overcome by active intervention, that is by requiring the repetition. Thus we finally come to the point of attributing *the chief rôle in analytic technique to repetition instead of to remembering.* This however, must not be understood as simply permitting effects to vanish away into "events," but consists rather, as is described in detail further on, in a gradual *transformation of the reproduced material into actual remembering* (first permitting the reproduction and then explaining it).

The progress which we could establish, by thus taking stock of our knowledge, can be observed and formulated into two headings. From the technical point of view we undoubtedly emphasize greater "activity," by which we mean absolutely requiring the tendency to reproduce, which has up to now been neglected, indeed regarded as a disturbing secondary phenomena in the cure. From the theoretic side, we lay stress on the adequate recognition in the neurosis also of the overwhelming importance of the

---

[2] In which case, this tendency frequently enough expresses itself in reality; this applies particularly to the love life, to marriage, divorce and love affairs, which are subjected to the greatest privation in the analysis.

repetition compulsion, which Freud has meantime established.[3] It is really the insight gained from understanding the repetition compulsion which first makes the results of "active therapy" comprehensible and gives the theoretic reason for its necessity. We therefore believe that we are in no way differing from Freud if from now on we attribute to repetition the same rôle in our therapy which it biologically occupies in our mental life.

[3] Beyond the Pleasure Principle. 1921.

CHAPTER II.

1. The Unwinding of the Libido and its Phases.*

If we now attempt to sketch, in broad outlines, the present stand of the therapy which is used in analysis, we would like, from the start, to have understood that we are not giving a detailed presentation of technique. In so far as this is at all possible in literary form, the task must be left for some work of quite a different character.[4] On the basis of the Freudian definition of psycho-analytic technique, which characterizes it as a method taking the mental facts of transference and resistance as the fundamental condition for the influencing of the patient, we can reach a very general definition of psycho-analysis which presents itself, at times, to the analyst conducting the treatment, *as an individually determined process of definite duration in the libido development of the patient.* The task of the analyst consists in watching the process of the automatic unwinding of the libido—which, like the organic process of healing, takes place within a definite time and contains crises. At those points where he notices a disturbance in the process in the form of a neurotic resistance he must intervene and correct it. This artificial libido process is inaugurated and determined in its course

---

* *Libido-ablauf* is here translated as *unwinding*—in the sense that as thread is unwound from a spool, so the libido is released or flows from the initial fixation stages by reason of the transference.

4 Moreover, instead of a written presentation of analytic technique, the aim should be a well and minutely worked out plan of instruction in psycho-analytic polyclinics. This would offer the only way of properly learning correct technique.

by the transference, which Ferenczi[5] described as a special instinct of the common human desire for transference, which expresses itself unusually strongly in the neurotic and merely occurs in the analysis under particularly favorable conditions. Whereas in real life this expansion of the libido is subject to inhibition and disturbance, the analysis permits this unwinding under certain conditions, indeed, at times, it even demands it. From this interpretation, the rôle of the analyst came to be generally understood as that of a passive agent who only occasionally intervened at a few points. He had in regard to the suffering of his patient to do nothing else than to permit him to express it, not only in order to see wherein it consisted, *i.e.*, "analytic diagnosis," but on account of certain peculiarities of the neurosis itself which presumes a revival of the old repressed material of the illness before a cure can be effected. Indeed the general practitioner can only interfere to correct an organic illness by concentrating and localizing the process of the disease. The analyst can learn from the general practitioner quiet, trained observation of the course of the illness, patience and an attitude of trusting somewhat to "nature." All the other virtues, often very valuable in a physician, may even interfere with the analytic work. The essential difference 'between the physician and the analyst, we can, according to Freud, formulate thus: the analyst not only uses the transference, which exists everywhere in a latent form, for the purpose of making the process of unwinding the libido easier, but also points out to the patient the transference at every step in order finally to free him from it. The last point seems to be one particularly contrary to the medical ideal,

[5] Introjektion und Uebertragung, Jahrbuch, 1909. See Sex in Psychoanalysis (Richard Badger, Boston, 1916).

since a large part of all medical art rests on the confidence of the patient, which the physician must maintain in the interest of the latter, *i.e.*, on the unconscious transference. From this point of view many more cures in internal medicine, which must use the unconscious transference as one of its most helpful weapons, are "the results of suggestion" than in psycho-analysis, for although psycho-analysis works with transference, it uses the resolution of this relationship as a therapeutic means to release the infantile libido fixation at the end of the treatment. Therefore the "ideal case," in analytic in contrast to medical practice, is that of the patient who having once been treated is never seen again, best cured when one never hears from him again. This result, however, presupposes a power of sublimation and renunciation on the part of the patient such as is not given to all people.

This interpretation of psycho-analysis, as an artificially induced process of the unwinding of the libido, for the purpose of correcting neurotic forms of discharge, answers automatically the frequent question as to the attitude of the analyst; his task is to remain rather passive in the face of the repetition of the libido overflow and to act as it were as the object or rather the phantom of the process. On the other hand, where a correction of the neurotic process is necessary he must certainly intervene "actively," behaving, so to speak, as a sort of catalyzer.

Before we answer the question how the analysis of the libidinal resistance is actually carried out, and what in general the points are at which the neurotic material presents itself for correction, we wish to emphasize that the phases of an analysis as given in the following description naturally do not occur thus schematically in actual practice. The principal question is how one deals with the phases of resistance and transference, the mastery of which takes place in the main work of the analysis which we might briefly call a libido privation cure.

In the phase of resistance in which the ego defends itself on the one hand against the unconscious itself, on the other hand, even more against the analysis of the unconscious, the material which appears is principally the preconscious memory material of the patient, or the manifest characteristics and ideals which his ego represents. All these "resistances," varying greatly in importance, which affect the course of the libido transference in the way we have described, are analyzed step by step during the analysis. Mostly the narcissistic resistances, proceeding from the ego, and the ideal formation appear at first; these are particularly difficult to overcome, because the patient, with the full weight of his whole actual personality, opposes the automatic unwinding of the libido attempted by his unconscious. Frequently the overcoming of these ego resistances only succeed after wounding the narcissism of the patient, or by means of a temporary suspension of his old ego ideal, after which the unwinding of the libido, or more correctly put, the affective expression of the libidinal instincts and desires proceeds more freely than before. From the phenomena of the transference, which represents, as it were, a replica of the infantile libido situation of the patient, we succeed in reproducing the disturbed infantile development of the individual by means of transforming the well known expressions of the unconscious into the language of consciousness, and also by means of the tendency to repeat old situations of the libido.

In the phase of resistance we have to deal with the preconscious memory material which the patient, under the influence of the analytic situation, so to speak, collects

out of his varied spheres of interest and centers of cathexis.[5a] In the phase of transference—in contrast to that of
resistance—it is always a question of making conscious the
tendency of the libido, operating in the transference, to
reproduce situations which mostly were never conscious at
all, but resulted from those tendencies and impulses which
were partly experienced in the infantile development, but
were at once repressed. By analyzing in the transference
these, as it were abortive wishes, which continue to struggle
for fulfillment in the unconscious but which the ego has
long since discarded (neurotic conflict) we give the patient
the opportunity to "experience" these wishes intensely
for the first time, in order, with the help of the conviction
which he thus acquires, and avoiding the formation of
pathological reactions, to place him in the position of
attaining an adjustment to reality. The chief resistance,
which has to be overcome in this process, is infantile
anxiety, or the uniting of this anxiety with the libidinal
parental conflict as an unconscious sense of guilt. The
latter in itself already contains sources of conflict, since it
results from the struggle of the ego ideal with the libidinal
tendencies and the wishes which correspond to them. The
neurotic indeed suffers, as the classical example of the
obsessional neurosis demonstrates, but as can clearly be
recognized in every other form of pathological mentality,
such as the perversions or the psychoses, etc., from an
overmeasure of this unconscious sense of guilt. If one
can succeed in reducing this sense of guilt, which operates
out of the repressed material, to a normal amount by in
part solving and abreacting it in fear, the libidinal

[5a] Cathexis-Besetzung, of original, is the technical term for libido "invest-
ment," or "charge" of libido. In electrical terms this is analogous to
"voltage" or "amperage" or a combination of both.

tendencies, which this sense of guilt have kept in check and suppressed since childhood, venture forth in the form of the transference. They can then be made conscious, and can, as the result of the analytic insight, be elaborated by the actual ego in a new and more useful way. It is well known that this new elaboration can result partly by means of repudiation, the erection of a new ego ideal, partly it can take the form of sublimation, a part can be allowed to express itself.[6]

The fact of creating the analytic situation in itself means giving full play for a time, if only in the phantasy of the transference libido, to those satisfactions which had up to then been rejected by the ego. Having done this, the analysis must now, by deciphering the reproduction presented in the transference, not only recognize the fixation of the infantile libido of the patient, but also by simultaneously freeing the libido from the predominance of the sense of guilt and anxiety for the first time provide a discharge. Since, in every case, it is also a question of reëxperiencing, of reproducing in contrast to remembering the preconscious material, the patient will naturally attempt to withdraw certain, for him, highly valuable libidinal situations from analytic reproduction by means of actual repetition. This must, of course, be recognized and prevented as far as possible, in extreme cases even by active intervention such as forbidding. It is different with analytic repetition which offers the opportunity, not only to reproduce certain situations in the analysis, but also to understand them analytically and to learn to control them. The conscious enlightenment of the patient during the

---

[6] This living out, or expressing itself of the libido, must not be understood to have any particular purpose. It is merely natural that a part of the freed libido of the neurotic should be accessible for direct satisfaction and need not be given up, since it belongs to normal life.

process often shows itself to be only a means of helping to reproduce repressed situations which cannot be "remembered" as such because, as we have said, they never had been conscious. In addition to giving the patient the idea of what he must expect in connection with his associations and resistances, the privation of libido is of essential assistance in attaining the reproduction. The patient must be subjected to this privation during the analysis, since the neurosis developed under the withdrawal of a libidinal satisfaction which he had previously enjoyed. By means of this libido privation one prevents a premature evaporation of the affects in the transference situation, and forces the libido back, at the same time analyzing and demonstrating these attempts, to the point from which the wrong development began, i.e., where the fixation occurred.

When the patient has in this way been freed from the repression, from anxiety and the feeling of guilt, and has with our "active" help found the courage to recognize his libidinal tendencies, the next step is to free the whole infantile libido, which has been reproduced in the transference, from the analytic situation, and to enable the patient to put it to a new and more normal use. This task occupies a particular phase of the analysis which we have called the weaning from the libido, and which analytically means the correct resolution of the transference. That the patient is ready for this is shown by decisive signs of various sorts which cannot be misunderstood. The chief characteristic of this situation, which has already been pointed out by Freud, is that the analysis has taken the place of the old neurosis in the form of an artificial neurosis—the actual libido fixation has taken the place of the infantile one—the analysis itself has, so to speak, become a compulsion. It is then merely a question, after adequately

working through this artificial transference neurosis, of re-
solving it and its new, actual tendency to fixation, a process
which takes place by diminishing the transference and
which must proceed just as slowly as the automatic unwinding of the libido under the suppression of the ego
resistances of the first phase. In this gradual development
and resolution of the analytic situation, the nature of the
analysis as a displacement, or demarcation of the libido
requiring a certain time to run its course can be seen
clearly.

At this point in the analysis when the libido development of the patient splits, so to speak, and is transferred
from the spool of the infantile fixation to that of the analytic
fixation, in the course of this unwinding at least all of the
pathologic fixations having been reproduced as it were on
a film, the intervention of the analyst in the matter of duration of the analysis takes place. He sets a definite period
of time for completing the last part of the treatment in
which the libido of the patient, following an automatic
course, now shows the tendency to fix itself in the analysis
as a substitute for the neurosis.

In this last phase of the analysis, in which the patient
must show that he is able to stand the withdrawal of the
libido, new resistances proceeding from the ego naturally
appear, which take the form of a depreciation of the whole
analytic work, and an unwillingness to accept its results,
since the unconscious of the patient had become adjusted to
accepting the analysis only if it received libidinal satisfaction in the transference. This must now be given up and
the results of the analysis and the attendant changes in the
attitude must nevertheless be accepted. This constitutes a
test of patience for the patient, who, from the very nature
of the neurotic privation, attempts to show that the with-

drawal of the libido places the cure in jeopardy, whereas it is in fact the only way in which the analytic task can be successfully completed. The period fixed for terminating the analysis after the transference neurosis has been established must be adhered to exactly, and one should not be misled by the "progress" which the patient, under the pressure of this inflexibility, may appear to make, into dismissing him earlier, for it is only in this very last phase that all those things which are decisive for the therapeutic result, and to which the earlier phases were only preparatory can be accomplished.

We can now, after glancing back, summarize the actual meaning of the analytic treatment as follows: the essential of the analysis consists, as we have said, in an unwinding process of the libido within a definite space of time, in the course of which all the demands of the infantile libido find a partial fulfillment in the transference; in reality, however, these demands, simultaneously with their being granted a sort of phantasy satisfaction, experience a gradual resolution culminating in their conscious adjustment. This interpretation of analysis, taking into consideration the contents and relations of the libido reactions which Freud has clearly worked out, of the procedure in analytic treatment and the analytic situations in which it culminates, suggests the following fundamental conception.

By placing the libido of the patient in the infantile parental relationship we make it possible for his actual personality, so to speak, to gradually change back to its first infantile condition. Accordingly the first phase of the analysis is taken up with this new attitude, or more correctly expressed, this revived attitude of the patient in which he catches up, so to speak, with the cathexes of all the highly developed ramifications of his ego system, of his personality, or of his neurosis, in order to lead them back into the track of the old Oedipus libido and its preliminary stages. This is the unconscious goal which guides the patient, and which we see, as if from a great distance, through all his associations, as well as in the inhibitory utterances of his resistances. The whole process takes place under tremendous pressure from the infantile libido, which has finally caught sight of the possibility of some sort of satisfaction, and proceeds under the protest of the whole actual personality which, with its ego ideal and pseudo-narcissistic tendencies, resists this reduction to the infantile. The more intensive the pressure of the libidinal tendencies to express themselves in the transference the greater are the inhibitive resistances of the ego. Here what we mean, when we say that actually we need only eliminate the resistances which stand in the way of the development of the libido transference, becomes clear. One must say fortunately, for otherwise the analytic efforts would be simply destroyed by the force and directness of the libidinal current. But the *real resistance, far from disturbing the analytic work* is actually a requisite and acts as a mainspring in regulating its course. On the other hand one must not think that the function of the resistance is solely to regulate the course of the libido and thus make the analysis possible at all; the content of the resistance is also of importance for it almost always is a sign that the patient here, too, reproduces instead of remembers and in the material betrays also that which he would like by means of reproduction to withdraw from analytic elaboration. From this point of view the resolution of the libidinal resistances by means of the analytic situation is one of the chief accomplishments of psychoanalytic technique.

When the first adjustment to the analytic situation has

succeeded, that is when the analyst has taken the place of the libidinal ego ideal—the father or the mother—then the original neurosis which proceeded from the Oedipus situation and which was displaced from this basis by the constantly increasing repression must artificially be led back to its original source. In doing this the transference becomes fully established in the sense of the unconscious, and is now used for the purpose of transforming the old Oedipus neurosis, which, under the influence of the ego development, had taken on the aspect of one of the familiar clinical forms, into a new analytical transference neurosis. *The resolution of this then takes place by means of consistently translating the unconscious material in all of its expressions, and their interpretations not only according to the meaning of the analytic situation, but also according to the infantile,* which runs parallel with it. In this way, by experiencing and living through to the end for the first time the infantile libidinal wishes, and continual settlement in the sense of making them conscious under privation, the patient finally learns to give up for good the unadjusted realization, and the pathologic satisfaction, of his infantile libido which is now critically cast aside by his new ego ideal. This is the reëducation to which the neurotic must subject his libido in the analysis. It takes place by permitting the patient gradually, by way of the transference, to regress to the period of the development of the "Oedipus complex" (not into the situation itself) and by enlightening him about this while removing the resistances, making the channels and ways of discharge which had been shut off open and accessible.

The correct and consistent execution of this task contains the most important technical problems of the psychoanalysis. For the particular way in which the normal

Oedipus libido is elaborated (mostly repressed) by the ego expresses itself in every individual case in the phenomena of transference and resistance, which must be understood, correctly reëstablished and then resolved. In the process certain typical forms of expression have naturally come to be recognized by repeated analytic experience, and have left their precipitate upon the theory, just as there are typical ways in which the ego attempts to master the libido, creating neurotic types or character types.

One reaction to the reproduction of the Oedipus situation in the analysis which seems to occur quite regularly is the manifestation of the castration complex. This, in the case of the man, means the turning away of the libido from the mother as object, and the identification with her, from which, according to the fate of the repression of the sense of guilt, operating as a motive power, the most various pathologic forms [7] can develop. In the case of the woman we see the turning away from the father, and the identification with him, in the sense of keeping the infantile wish for a penis. Just as in the infantile development this mechanism is intended to serve the purpose of avoiding the Oedipus rôle so in the analysis, which again calls forth this situation, the castration complex appears, so to speak, as a "negative Oedipus complex". Thus what we find in the analysis as the "castration complex" corresponds to a neurotic application (defense sympton) of the normal infantile bisexuality, that is a stage of development in which there was as yet no differentiation of the sexes. Naturally this symptom points back to the deeper infantile stages of development common to both sexes, which cannot here be further discussed. [8]

[7] See Rank "Perversion and Neurosis".
[8] See now Rank "Das Trauma der Geburt". 1924.

Taking as our point of departure the already greatly distorted neurosis, as it becomes manifest in the clinical symptoms, we place the patient in the transference neurosis and thus enable him to experience in the analysis the never actually active "original neurosis" of the Oedipus complex with all its preliminary stages. This makes his illness, which was intended to replace these inaccessible repressed original expressions, useless. The two periods of the analytic intervention, the activation of the original neurosis and its resolution appear to correspond to the two periods of the development of the neurosis, the infantile neurosis and the clinical neurosis, which themselves again follow, according to Freud's elucidation, the biological facts of the two periods of sexual development characteristic of man.[9]

The neurosis is characterized by the projection into the phase of maturity, of the first, from its very nature incomplete and also incompletely overcome, phase of sexual development and repression. In his unconscious the neurotic remains therefore at a primitive biologic stage of conflict, which explains the infantile character of the neuroses as well as the necessity for analytic reëducation. Therefore not only is there a childhood neurosis back of every neurosis, but it is the direct task of the analysis to uncover the infantile neurosis back of the clinical neurosis, that is, to reduce the clinical neurosis to its conflicting preliminary stages, even if these have never been manifest. This original neurosis can only be repeated by means of reproduction in the analysis, principally experienced in the transference and thus psychically eliminated.

[9] We here see the rare occurrence that a point of view which developed from practical (theoretical) necessity can later be used as the confirmation of an earlier theoretic assumption and not merely as a mechanical application of the same.

Psychoanalysis thus allows the patient to relive, partly even for the first time to live through to the end, the original infantile libidinal situation with a partial satisfaction under the condition of consciously giving up its unadjusted realization. This task can, under the pressure of the analysis, be executed by the adult ego of the patient so that he is able consciously to stand the unrequited Oedipus love. Indeed it is this ability to stand a partial giving up, at the same time avoiding an en bloc repression; which on the whole enables a person to seize the possibilities of substitute satisfactions which reality offers. In the analysis the infantile love impulses, which live on in the unconscious, suppressed in their development, struggle to repeat themselves, or they are brought to the surface with the help of our technique. *Thus in the correctly executed analysis the whole development of the individual is not repeated, but only those phases of development of the infantile libido on which the ego, in spite of their uselessness, has remained fixed.*

The theoretic question whether the analysis is an education of the ego, or an education of the libidinal instincts, can in practice be answered somewhat in this way. The first phase of every analysis represents an education of the ego, in so much as it accustoms the ego of the patient to recognize expressions of the libido contrary to the ego, and prevents the repetition of the old process of repression. In a later phase, after the transference has developed, the libido, the development of which was arrested in childhood, fully unfolds; in the weaning, or phase of deprivation, the ego energy or forces proceeding from the new ego ideal again see to it that the newly awakened desires adjust themselves to reality. Naturally these ego forces do not need to be thrust upon the patient by any sort of moral

talk or by giving him anagogic goals, for they exist from
the first in every patient who is not insane just as much as
the desire for transference. Indeed it is these ego forces
which finally bring about the process of cure, the further
transference of the libido from the analyst to "more real
objects" in life or which makes it possible to stand unsatisfied, free floating libido. Without the help of these ego
forces, and without some natural egoism, the final task of
psycho-analysis, the weaning from the cure, would be impossible. For in this phase the problem is to get the
patient, with the help of the love for the analyst, to give up
this love. This would be a contradiction in terms and quite
an impossibility if the intelligence of the patient did not
assist. After the patient has become convinced that he
cannot obtain the love of the analyst in reality—and that
such is the case he only admits in the very last phase of the
cure—he recognizes, consciously as well as emotionally, the
impossibility of fulfilling the demands of his infantile
libido and contents himself with the other things which life
offers. It is remarkable with what haste the libido, as it
frees itself from the cure, seeks out new interests in life.
We see the process of sublimation which in ordinary life
requires years of education, take place before our eyes
towards the end of the cure in the shortest space of time,
without any particular guidance being necessary. The
libido which has become available spontaneously seizes
every opportunity, every possibility of discharge for expressing itself in a way compatible with its ego.

*II. The Freeing of the Libido Fixation in the Factor
of Experience.*

The creation of the analytic situation really exposes the
patient a second time to his infantile trauma by offering

his unsatisfied Oedipus libido, which had displaced itself neurotically upon inadequate objects, the actual old object. The discharge of libidinal excitation thus inaugurated, represents for the unconscious of the patient a satisfaction which he is not able to find anywhere else in life, and which binds him to the situation. We give the patient the parental imago which he has sought from earliest childhood and on which he can emotionally live out his libido. The patient, by identifying us with his father or mother, shows clearly that it is this ideal parental imago which he seeks, which we, however, cannot offer him permanently in the form in which he wishes it. However, if we did so, we would, as frequently enough happens, apparently "cure" the patient by making him happily in love, whereas the analysis must aim to get him to give up a part of this infantile libido by realizing that its satisfaction is unattainable. We have finally to show him by a painful experience, so to speak, that the fulfillment of his wishes would be contrary to his adult ego ideal and in what manner.

During and by means of the transference the erection of a new temporary ideal takes place; the ego ideal, which the patient has brought with him, defends itself against the provisional ideal in the form of resistances, whereas his old repressed infantile nature struggles for it. By acting at first, as Freud expressed it, as the champion of the repressed material one is able to clear away the resistances proceeding from the ego. One of the most frequent manifestations of the resistance, in the beginning of the analysis, is the identification with the father, with the obstinate wish to surpass him in everything which opposes the acceptance of the infantile situation presented by the analysis. This first phase of the analysis of the ego resistances sometimes already requires the active intervention of the analyst which, however, need not go beyond the rôle of the analytical parental authority which is given by the transference. When the ego resistances have been cleared away and the transference fully and adequately established, it is used for the reproduction in the analysis, until finally the libido resistance, which is the second big resistance after the ego resistance, develops out of the transference, which means the natural striving against the necessarily enforced privation. It is only at this point that the transference which up to now has been a means of promoting the analysis becomes its object and must be explained to the patient as such.

In general one must not estimate too highly the direct therapeutic value of explanations which do not directly serve to clear away resistance. One need not even think of the well known type of the obsessional neurotic who, after a lengthy analysis, has the whole analytic knowledge of his analyst in his little finger, and can even surpass him in analyzing his own symptoms without having been in the least helped in regard to his suffering. No matter how much such a patient has learned from his analyst, and even understood, he has not yet experienced anything which has brought this "knowledge" home to him. But one does not have to go so far to see an example of the therapeutic uselessness of this "mere knowledge". It is sufficient to think of those people who somehow—mostly out of neurotic motives—have come to practice psycho-analysis only to realize after a few failures that they need analysis themselves. Such persons generally come to the treatment with more or less ready knowledge—even of their own symptoms—which as they themselves demonstrate could not prevent them from becoming the victim of a neurosis and was not able to free them from it. On the contrary for such analysts the practice of psycho-analysis seems to have been a symptom of their own neuroses, in so far as the analysis reactivated the old Oedipus situation for themselves, which they are therefore never in a position to fully resolve in their patients.[10] The analysis of such persons would be an instructive object lesson for beginning analysts and would probably save them from certain technical mistakes. For they would then find themselves confronted by a patient whose theoretical knowledge of analysis was somewhat commensurate with their own, and would therefore be placed before the task of discovering that the therapeutic influencing of a patient is something in its very nature entirely different from the mere imparting of theoretical knowledge. By comparing such analyses with those of more naïve patients one can best recognize that *all enlightenment and explanation alone is only a first help in making* clear to the patient the meaning of the reproduction that he is to expect in the analytical experience. One need in no way fear that the patient will be "frightened" by a premature explanation and fall into a state of resistance. Of course there are situations in the analysis in which not interpreting is the proper reaction in order to get from the patient all the material belonging to a certain situation, whereas by a premature interpretation in such a case the last unconscious motive of the often very important connecting links may get lost.[11] If the analyst does not understand and control the analytical situation he cannot

10 We have indeed found from experience that some supporters, while consciously recognizing analysis, simply reacted with their latent neurosis out of which they then created their resistances in the form of scientific objections.

11 It would be somewhat as if one were to interpret the loosing of an object symbolically as "castration" without paying any attention to the finer mechanics of the slip (such as sacrifice or sense of guilt).

do anything except let the patient "associate" and "interpret" to him the single associations. The protraction of this method reduces the analysis to the level of an association experiment as if the point were to prove to the patient that he has complexes and which ones.

It is the fundamental rule of analytic technique, that the analyst should only come out from his shell of observational reserve, from the rôle of merely existing, when it is absolutely necessary, that is in general when the resistances require him to intervene in the unwinding of the libido in the way which we have above indicated. As much as possible this should occur only in the few big and really decisive situations of the analysis, whereas one should carefully avoid trying to be overconscientious about interpreting details, or wishing to understand at once everything that the patient says or does and to explain it to him. Such excess of zeal means disregarding the fact, which is also of theoretic importance, that the associations are often only brought forward by the patient for some purpose and this must then be made conscious to the patient instead of losing oneself in the details of interpreting single associations. The same considerations must be observed to an even greater degree in the interpretation of dreams which, in the practical analysis, need not be carried out as though the point were to prove the correctness of theory,[12] but so as to take out of the dream what corresponds in importance to the analytic situation. Otherwise one falls into the disastrous mistake of neglect-

---

[12] Meantime Freud's work *Zur Theorie und Praxis der Traumdeutung* (Zeitschrift IX, 1, 1913) which belongs here has appeared.

"Analyses of dreams" occasionally published with pride which have been "worked" upon many hours are not very good evidence for the analyst, no matter what interesting material such studies may give for the psychology of dreams or the technique of the interpretation.

ing the actual task for the sake of the psychological interest. This consists in understanding and interpreting every expression of the patient above all as a reaction to the present analytical situation (defense against, or recognition of the exposition of the analyst, emotional reactions to these, etc.), in doing which it is important to differentiate between what is actually provoked and infantile repetition, or at times to understand and get the patient to recognize what is common to both.

This holds for every separate symptom, for every dream, even for the understanding of the separate associations, but above all for the whole analytical situation. Thus it becomes particularly important to analyze the unconscious conditions which have brought the patient to the analysis, as well as the conditions and requirements which he associates with the end of the analysis, among these particularly conditions as to the length of time (for example when the patient from the first wishes to set a definite date for finishing). Such an attitude, if it is not disposed of from the first, can defeat the final result of an analysis, no matter how well it has been carried out in the details. The previous exposition shows clearly how the original abreacting of the affects—in spite of all the increase in our knowledge—has actually still remained the essential therapeutic agent, with, however, the important advance that we no longer leave the course to be determined by the compulsion to repeat and also no longer restrict it to one single "jammed in" affect. The tremendous difference between the abreaction in catharsis and that in the "psycho-analytical experience," according to our meaning, is that in catharsis one tried to provoke the discharge of the affects in direct connection with the reawakening of the pathological memory traces, whereas our present day analytic technique allows the affects which are pathological in their working to run off, or to be provoked in the relation to the analyst, or the analysis, that is in the analytic situation, first using these affective expressions in order spontaneously to bring to memory or to reproduce[13] the traumatic factors of the past.

In the difference here given, between seeking memories for the purpose of reaching the affects and provoking the affects for the sake of uncovering the unconscious, we can see the deepest causes why psycho-analysis as a science had first to go through a phase of understanding before it could come to a full appreciation of the factor of experience.

Only at this point can we understand and solve the apparent contradiction between Freud's interpretation of the predominating importance of remembering and our emphasis on experience and on its reproduction. The tendency, which we also pursue, of provoking the repetition in the analytical situation finally ends by creating for the patient, so to speak, new actual memories in place of the pathological complexes shut off from the rest of the mental content. These pathologic complexes are reawakened and translated into "remembering" by being made conscious during the experience without permitting the time and possibility for "repression." Thus in the end remembering still remains the final factor of healing and the actual problem is constantly to transform one—as it were organic—kind of repeating, the reproducing, into another mental form of repeating, the remembering, which itself is only a form of the mnemonic repetition-compulsion. In this proc-

[13] See Ferenczi: Weitere Beiträge zur aktiven Technik in der Psychoanalyse (Zeitschrift, 1921). Now and again a spontaneous "cathartic" discharge takes place generally in connection with not very deeply repressed memory material.

ess it becomes clear why just the analytic privation, which represents as it were a repetition of the trauma for the patient, is indispensable in obtaining the conviction necessary to the cure. Indeed to consciously become aware of anything is, in general, a mental phenomenon which human beings never produce except under the pressure of a privation-situation, that is in order to avoid pain. The note of conviction is missing about knowledge[14] acquired in any other way, no matter how compelling it may be in point of logic.

Therefore we must force the individual in the analysis to reproduce the essentially unconscious part of his faulty development, allowing him to live out a part of the libido which had been deprived of satisfaction, under the condition that he, by discharging it, and at the same time by insight into its mechanisms, gives up the false adjustment, and on the basis of a new advance in development, substitutes a more real adjustment. This takes place by leading the course of excitation from the unconscious phantasies to the higher preconscious thinking in the analytical situation. This for the first time paves the way for a discharge of the affects and thus raises the whole mental existence to a different level, that of adjustment to reality. A correctly executed psycho-analysis is from this point of view a social process, a "mass structure of two," according to an utterance of Freud, in which the analyst must take the place of the whole heterogeneous environment, particularly of the most important persons in the surroundings of the patient.

[14] See Ferenczi: *Introjektion und Übertragung*, Jahrbuch I, 1909.

CHAPTER III.

Now that we have in a brief outline described what we mean by the psycho-analytic method, we are able to look back and to recognize that a series of mistakes in the technique correspond to remaining stationary at certain stages of development in analytic perception. It is only natural that such inhibitions in development not only were possible and occurred in all the phases of the analytic progress, but also that they still exist, or repeat themselves to-day.

We wish not only to show in individual points how this is to be interpreted, and thus to throw a side light on the historic development of psycho-analysis, but also principally to help to avoid such faulty developments in the future. What now follows is actually the presentation of a series of incorrect methods, that is of such as no longer correspond to an up-to-date conception of the psycho-analytic technique.

In view of the general clinical, phenomenalistic point of view in medicine, it is not to be wondered at that in the medical practice of psycho-analysis a kind of descriptive analysis, actually a contradiction in terms, was reached. Such an analysis, as a rule, limited itself to listening, or to an expansive description of the symptoms, or the perverse wishes of the patient, without any essential therapeutic effect resulting from this mere "talking out," because the dynamic factor of experience was neglected.

A similarly misunderstood kind of analysis consisted in the collecting of associations, as if these were in themselves the essential thing, and not merely rising bubbles of consciousness showing us where, or perhaps at what depth under the surface, the active affects were concealed, and particularly what motives drove the patient in a given case to use the ways of association which he seemed to prefer.

Less harmless was the fanaticism for interpreting, which resulted in overlooking, in a cut and dried translation according to the dictionary, the fact that the technique of interpretation is but one of the means of help in understanding the unconscious mental condition of the patient, and not the aim, or certainly not the chief aim, of the analysis. This translation of the associations of the patient is of the same value as in the realm of language from which the comparison is taken. The unavoidable preliminary work to the understanding of the whole text, is the looking up of unknown words, but it is not an aim in itself. This "translation" must be followed by the "interpretation", so as to give a comprehensible connection. Viewed from this angle, the frequent disputes over the correctness of an interpretation, *i.e.*, translation, disappear. Questions from analysts whether this or that "interpretation"—in our sense of the word translation is meant—be correct or the query what this or that, perhaps in a dream, "means", show an incomplete understanding of the whole analytic situation and an overestimation, such as we have just pointed out, of isolated details. These can mean sometimes one thing, sometimes another. The same symbol in the same patient can have, or take on, a different meaning under the pressure or the loosening of a resistance. In an analysis fine details, apparent incidentals such as voice, gesture, expression, are so important. So much depends upon the successful interpolation, upon the comprehensible relationship, upon the meaning which the expressions of the patient acquire by his own unconscious commentary with the help of our interpretation. Thus the technique of translation forgot in the interest of the "correct" translation of details, that the whole, that is the analytic situation of the patient as such, also has a meaning, and indeed the chief meaning. Only from an understanding of the whole can the correct interpretation of the translated parts follow; this is then free and certain, whereas the fanaticism of translation leads to mere routine work and is therapeutically fruitless.

Another faulty method was holding fast to the already overcome phase of the analysis of the symptoms. It is well known that there was an early period of psychoanalysis in which, by proceeding from the separate symptoms, and by suggestive pressure those memories were called forth, which, working in the unconscious, produced the symptoms. On account of the later development in the psychoanalytic technique this method has long been given up. It is, indeed, not even a question of getting the symptoms to disappear, which every suggestive method can easily accomplish, but rather preventing their return, which means making the ego of the patient more capable of resistance. For this purpose an analysis of the whole personality is necessary. The analyst should, according to Freud's direction, always proceed from what is at the time the mental surface and must not pursue the associative connections with the symptoms. Evidently it was too tempting and easy to obtain information about the neurotic, or perverse behavior of the patient by directly asking him and thus let him directly remember the history of the development of his abnormality.[15] Only a series of converg-

---

[15] This rejection of the principle of the "analysis of symptoms" naturally does not preclude at times asking the patient the reason for the particular obtrusiveness of some symptomatic expression (for example the so-called temporary symptoms).

ing experiences can place us in the position of understanding the many "interpretations" which one symptom can have in a particular case. Direct questions merely succeeded in turning the attention of the patient towards this factor at the wrong time, thus establishing his resistances at this point, for the patient was able to misuse this, in itself, not entirely unjustified direction of his attention. Thus it could happen that the "analysis" was unduly protracted, but the original infantile story, without the reconstruction of which no treatment can be called a real analysis, was never reached.

We must deal, somewhat more in detail, with one phase of analysis which can be called the "analysis of complexes" and which preserves an important stage of the amalgation with academic psychology. The word "complex" was first used by Jung as the simplification of a complicated psychological fact, to designate certain tendencies, characteristic for the person in question, or a related group of affect-colored conceptions. This interpretation of the word which was constantly becoming more comprehensive, and had thus come to have almost no meaning, was then limited by Freud who described the *unconscious repressed parts* of those group conceptions with the name "complex." As the more subtle, labile, fluctuating processes of cathexis in the psyche became accessible to research, the acceptance of such inflexible, separate mental components became more and more superfluous. They were too coherent, they could only be excited and displaced in toto, they were much too "complex," as more exact analysis showed, to be treated as elements which could not be further reduced. Indeed in the newer works of Freud, this conception merely figures as the survival of a period of psycho-analysis, for which we have actually no more use, especially since the creation of our meta-psychology.

The most consistent thing would have been to have done away entirely with this now useless rudiment of an earlier time, and to have given up the terminology, which had become dear to most analysts, in favor of a better understanding. Instead of doing this, the whole of mental life was often regarded as a mosaic of such complexes, and the analysis then carried out with the object of "analyzing out" one complex after the other, or the attempt was made of treating the whole personality as a sum total of father-mother-, brother-, and sister-complexes. It was naturally easy to collect material for these, since every one has, of course, all the complexes, that is, every one must, in the course of his development, somehow get on with the persons and objects which surround him. The connected recounting of complexes, or the attributes of these, may have its place in descriptive psychology, but not in the practical analysis of the neurotic, nor does it even belong in the psycho-analytic study of literary, or ethno-psychological products where it must undoubtedly lead to a monotony in no way justified by the many sidedness of the material, and which was scarcely tempered by giving preference, first to one and then to the other complex.

Although such a flattening out may have to be put up with at times, as unavoidable in a scientific presentation, one should not therefore transfer such a cramped interest into the technique. The analysis of complexes easily misleads the patient into being pleasing to his analyst, by bringing him "complex material" as long as he likes, without giving up any of his really unconscious secrets. Thus there came to be histories of illnesses in which the patients recounted memories, evidently fabricating them, in a way that never happens in unprejudiced analyses, and can only be looked upon as the product of such a "breeding of complexes." Such results should naturally not be used subjectively either to show the correctness of one's own method of interpreting, or as theoretic conclusions, nor yet as leading to any sort of evidence.[16]

It happened particularly frequently that the associations of the patient were directed to the sexual factor at the wrong time, or that they remained stuck at this point if—as so often happens—he came to the analysis with the expectation that he must constantly talk exclusively of his actual or infantile sexual life. Aside from the fact that this is not so exclusively the case as our opponents think, permitting such an indulgence in the sexual often gives the patient the opportunity to paralyze the therapeutic effect of the privation he must undergo.

An understanding of the many sided and important mental contents which underlie the collective name "castration complex" was also not exactly furthered by bringing the theory of the complexes into the dynamics of the analysis. On the contrary, we are of the opinion that the premature theoretic condensation of the facts under the conception of the complex interfered with the insight into deeper layers of mental life. We believe that the full appreciation of that which the analytic practitioner has accustomed himself to finish off with the label "castration complex" is still lacking, so that this attempt at an explanation should not lightly be regarded as the ultimate explanation of such varied mental phenomena and

[16] Stekel, who attributed the same neurotic symptom first to sexuality, then to crime and finally to religion, may be taken as an extreme example of the subjectivity of such a passion for complexes. He may in this way, since he asserted everything, possibly have been right in some one of his single utterances.

processes of the patient. We can, from the dynamic stand-point, which is the only justifiable one in practice, often recognize in the forms of expression of the castration complex, as they manifest themselves in the course of the analysis, only one of the kinds of resistance which the patient erects against his deeper libidinal wishes. In the early stages of some analyses the castration anxiety can often be uncovered as an expression of the dread, trans-ferred onto the analyst, as a protection against further analysis.

As we have already intimated, technical difficulties arose also from the analyst having too much knowledge. Thus the importance of the theory of sexual development con-structed by Freud, misled some analysts to apply in a mistaken and over-dogmatic fashion in the therapy of the neuroses, certain systems of organization and auto-eroticisms which first gave us an understanding of normal sexual development. In thus searching for the construc-tive elements of the theory of sex, in some cases, the actual analytic task was neglected. These analyses might be compared to psychochemical "element analyses." Here again one could see that the theoretical importance did not always correspond to the value in the practical analysis. The technique need not methodically lay bare all the, as it were, prescribed historic phases of the development of the libido, still less should the uncovering of all theoretically estabished details and gradations be used as a principle of healing in the neuroses. It is also practically superfluous to demonstrate all the original elements of a highly complicated "connection," while missing the intellectual thread, which combines the few fundamental elements into new and varying phenomena. The same thing holds for the erotogenic zones as for the complexes, for example the urethral or the anal erotic, and for the stages of organization the oral, anal-sadistic and other pregenital phases; there can be no human development without all of these, but one must not in the analysis attribute to them the importance, for the history of the illness, of which the resistance under the pressure of the analytic situation gives the illusion.

On closer observation a certain inner connection between "element analyses" and "complex-analyses" could be recognized, insofar as the latter, in their attempts to plumb the psychic depths, struck upon the granite of the complexes and thus the work was spread out over the surface instead of going to the bottom. Such analyses then usually tried to make up for the lack of depth in the dynamics of the libido by an excursion into the theory of sex, and united rigid attributes of complexes with equally schematically treated principles of the theory of sex, whereas they missed just the play of forces which takes place between the two.

Such an attitude naturally led to a theoretic overestimation of the factor of quantity, to ascribing everything to a stronger organ—eroticism, a point of view—which resembled that of the pre-analytical school of neurologists—who blinded themselves to any insight into actual play of forces of the pathological causes by the catch words "inheritance," "degeneration," "disposition."

Since the theory of the instincts and also the sciences of biology and physiology have been called upon partly as a help in understanding mental phenomena, in particular since the so-called "pathoneurosen," that is the neuroses on the organic level, the organ-neuroses, and even organic illnesses are treated psycho-analytically, disputes about border-line cases have taken place between psycho-analysis and physiology. The stereotyped translation of physiological processes into the language of psycho-analysis is incorrect. Insofar as one attempts to approach organic processes analytically the rules of psycho-analysis must be strictly adhered to here also. One must try to forget, so to speak, one's organic, medical and physiological knowledge and to bear in mind only the mental personality and its reactions.

It was also confusing when simple clinical facts were at once combined with speculations about becoming, being and duration and such deliberations treated like established rules in practical analysis, whereas Freud himself constantly emphasizes the hypothetical character of his last synthetic works. Often enough such a wandering into speculation seems to have been a dodging of uncomfortable technical difficulties. We know how a desire to prematurely condense everything under a speculative principle can wreak vengeance from the point of view of technique.[17] (The Jungian theory).

It was also a mistake, while neglecting the individual, in the explanation of the symptoms, to make cultural and phylogenetic analogies at once, no matter how fruitful the latter might be in themselves. On the other hand, the overestimate of the actual factors led to an anagogic prospective interpretation, which was useless so far as the pathologic fixations were concerned. The adherents of the "anagogic," as well as some of those of the "genetic" school, in their interest in the future and in the past,

[17] It is well known that Jung went so far as to neglect the mnemonic importance of the infantile experiences brought to light in the analysis and of the personalities playing an important part in them in favor of an analysis on the "subjective-level". It shows a high degree of flight from reality to be willing to acknowledge the existence and force of only the idealized, or much too impersonal conception, of the obscure derivations of the original memories of objects and of people.

neglected the present condition of the patient. And yet almost all of the past, and everything that the unconscious attempts, insofar as it is not directly conscious or remembered (and this occurs extremely seldom), expresses itself in actual reactions in relation to the analyst or to the analysis, in other words in the transference to the analytic situation.

The requirements of the Breuer-Freud catharsis that the affects, displaced upon symptoms, should be led back directly to the pathologic memory-traces, and at the same time brought to a discharge and bound again proved to be unrealizable, that is, it succeeds only in the case of incompletely repressed, mostly preconscious memory-material as in the case of certain derivatives of the actual unconscious. This itself, the uncovering of which is the chief task of the analysis, since it was never "experienced" can never be "remembered," one must let it be produced on the ground of certain indications. The mere communication, something like "reconstruction," is in itself not suited to call forth affect reactions; such information glides off from the patients without any effect. They can only convince themselves of the reality of the unconscious when they have experienced—mostly indeed only after they have frequently experienced—something analogous to it in the actual analytic situation, that is, in the present. Our new insight into the topography of mental life and the functions of the separate depth levels gives us the explanation for this state of affairs. The unconscious repressed material has no approach to motility, nor to those motor innervations in the sum total of which the affect discharge consists; the past and the repressed must find their representative factors in the present and the conscious (preconscious) in order that they may be affectively experienced and develop further. In contrast to the stormy abreaction one could designate the unwinding bit by bit of the affects in analysis as a fractional catharsis.

We believe, moreover, in general that affects in order to work convincingly must first be revived, that is made actually present and that what has not affected us directly and actually must remain mentally ineffective.

The analyst must always take into account that almost every expression of his patient springs from several periods, but he must give his chief attention to the present reaction. Only from this point of view can he succeed in uncovering the roots of the actual reaction in the past, which means changing the attempts of the patient to repeat into remembering. In this process he need pay little attention to the future. One may quietly leave this care to the person himself who has been sufficiently enlightened about his past and present mental strivings. The historic, cultural and phylogenetic analogies also need, for the most part, not be discussed in the analysis. The patient need hardly ever, and the analyst extremely seldom, occupy himself with this early period.

At this place we must consider certain misunderstandings about the enlightenment of people who are being analyzed. There was a phase, in the development of psycho-analysis, in which the goal of the analytic treatment consisted in filling the gaps in the memory of the patient with knowledge. Later one recognized that the neurotic ignorance proceeded from the resistance, that is from not wishing to know, and that it was this resistance which had to be constantly uncovered and made harmless. If one proceeds thus the amnesic gaps in the chain of memories fill themselves in, for the most part automatically, the other part with the help of sparse interpretations and explanations. The patient therefore learns nothing more and nothing other than what he needs, and in the quantity requisite to allay the predominating disturbances. It was a fatal mistake to believe that no one was completely analyzed who had not also been theoretically familiarized with all the separate details of his own abnormality. Naturally it is not easy to set a boundary line up to which the instruction of the patient should be carried. Interruption of the correct analysis by formal courses of instruction may satisfy both the analyst and the patient, but cannot effect any change in the libido-attitude of the sick person. A further result of such instruction was that, without noticing it, one pushed the patient into withdrawing himself from the analytical work by means of identifying himself with the analyst. The fact that the desire to learn and to teach creates an unfavorable mental attitude for the analysis is well known but should receive much more serious attention.[18]

At times one heard from analysts the complaint that this or that analysis failed on account of "too great resistances" or a too "violent transference." The possibility in principle of such extreme cases is admitted; we do find ourselves at times confronted with quantitative factors, which we must in no way practically underestimate, since they play an important part in the final outcome of the analysis, as well as in its causes. But the factor of quantity, so important in itself, can be used as a screen for incomplete insight into the play of forces which finally decide the kind of application and the distribution of

18 This holds also for persons who come to be analyzed only for the sake of learning (the so-called "didactic analyses"). In such cases it occurs only too easily that the resistances get displaced onto the intellectual field (science) and so remain unexplained.

those very quantities. Because Freud once uttered the sentence, "Everything which impedes the analytic work is resistance," one should not, every time the analysis comes to a standstill, simply say, "this is a resistance." This resulted, particularly in patients with an easily aroused sense of guilt, in creating an analytic atmosphere in which they, so to speak, were fearful of making the "faux pas" of having a resistance, and the analyst found himself in a helpless situation. One evidently forgot another utterance of Freud, namely, that in the analysis we must be prepared to meet the same forces, which formerly caused the repression as "resistances," as soon as one sets to work to release these repressions.

Another analytical situation which one was also in the habit of labelling incorrectly as "resistance" is the negative transference, which, from its very nature, cannot express itself otherwise than as "resistance" and the analysis of which is the most important task of the therapeutic activity. One need, of course, not be afraid of the negative reactions of the patient for they constitute, with iron necessity, a part of every analysis. Also the strong positive transference, particularly when it expresses itself in the beginning of the cure, is only a symptom of resistance which requires to be unmasked. In other cases, and particularly in the later stages of an analysis, it is an actual vehicle for bringing to light desires which have remained unconscious.

In this connection an important rule of psycho-analytic technique must be mentioned in regard to the personal relation between the analyst and the patient. The theoretic requirement of avoiding all personal contact outside of the analysis mostly led to an unnatural elimination of all human factors in the analysis, and thus again to a theorizing of the analytic experience.

From this point of view some practitioners all too readily failed to attribute that importance to a change in the person of the analyst, which results from the interpretation of the analysis as a mental process, the unity of which is determined by the person of the analyst. A change of analysts may be unavoidable for outer reasons in rare, exceptional cases, but we believe that technical difficulties—in homosexuals, for example—are not simply to be avoided by the choice of an analyst of the opposite sex. For in every correct analysis the analyst plays all possible rôles for the unconscious of the patient; it only depends upon him always to recognize this at the proper time and under certain circumstances to consciously make use of it. Particularly important is the rôle of the two parental images—father and mother—in which the analyst actually constantly alternates (transference and resistance).

It is not an accident that technical mistakes occurred so frequently just in the expression of transference and resistance. One was easily inclined to let oneself be surprised at these elementary experiences in the analysis and strangely enough forgot just here the theory which had been incorrectly pushed into the foreground in the wrong place. This may also be due to subjective factors in the analyst. The narcissism of the analyst seems suited to create a particularly fruitful source of mistakes; among others the development of a kind of narcissistic counter transference which provokes the person being analyzed into pushing into the foreground certain things which flatter the analyst and, on the other hand, into suppressing remarks and associations of an unpleasant nature in relation to him. Both are technically incorrect: the first because it can lead to an apparent improvement of the patient which is only intended to bribe the analyst and in this way to win a libidinal counter interest from him; the second because it keeps the analyst from the necessity of noticing the delicate indications of criticism, which mostly only venture forth hesitatingly, and helping the patient to express them plainly or to abreact them. The anxiety and the sense of guilt of the patient can never be overcome without this self-criticism, requiring indeed a certain overcoming of himself on the part of the analyst; and yet these two emotional factors are the most essential for bringing about and maintaining the repression.

Another form under which technical inaccessibility hid itself was an incidental remark of Freud to the effect that the narcissism of the patient could set limits to the degree to which he could be influenced by the analysis. If the analysis did not progress well, one consoled oneself with the thought that the patient was "too narcissistic." And since narcissism forms a connecting link between ego and libidinal strivings in all normal, as well as abnormal mental processes, it is not difficult to find proofs in his behavior and thoughts for the narcissism of the patient. Particularly one should not handle the narcissistically determined "castration" or "masculinity" complexes as if they set the limits for analytic solution.[19]

When the analysis struck upon a resistance of the patient one often overlooked to what extent a pseudo-narcissistic tendency was brought into the question. The analyses of people who bring a certain theoretic knowledge with them into their analyses are particularly

---

[19] We know that Adler, who evidently did not succeed in the analysis of the libido, remained stuck at this point.

calculated to convince one that a great deal of what one was theoretically inclined to ascribe to narcissism, is actually secondary, pseudo-narcissistic and can by continued analysis be completely solved in the parental relationship. Naturally it is necessary in doing this to take up analytically the ego-development of the patient, as indeed it is in general necessary in the analysis of the resistances to consider the up-to-now much too neglected analysis of the ego, for which Freud has recently given valuable hints.

The newness of a technical point of view introduced by Ferenczi under the name of "activity" resulted in some analysts, in order to avoid technical difficulties, overwhelming the patient with commands and prohibitions, which one might characterize as a kind of "wild activity." This, however, must be looked upon as a reaction to the other extreme, to holding too fast to an over-rigid "passivity" in the matter of technique. The latter is certainly sufficiently justified by the theoretic attitude of the analyst who must at the same time be an investigator. In practice, however, this easily leads to sparing the patient the pain of necessary intervention, and to allowing him too much initiative in his associations as well as in the interpretation of his ideas.[20]

The moderate, but, when necessary, energetic activity in the analysis consists in the analyst taking on, and, to a certain extent, really carrying out those rôles which the

---

[20] Patients with a strongly "masochistic" attitude are particularly fond of making use of an over "passive technique" on the part of the analysts by themselves undertaking interpretations on the "subjective level" by doing which they satisfy their tendency to torment themselves, at the same time opposing the deeper interpretation with a skeptical resistance. In the same way, one can, moreover, get any "anagogic" interpretation of dreams that one likes by letting somewhat instructed patients interpret the dream elements, without getting behind the dynamics of the resistance overcompensated by morality.

unconscious of the patient and his tendency to flight prescribe. By doing this the tendency to the repetition of earlier traumatic experiences is given an impetus, naturally with the goal of finally overcoming this tendency by revealing its content. When this repetition takes place spontaneously it is superfluous to provoke it and the analyst can simply call forth the transformation of the resistance into remembering (or plausible reconstruction).

These last purely technical remarks lead back to the often mentioned subject of the reciprocal effect of theory and practice about which we must now make some general methodological remarks.

CHAPTER IV.

THE RECIPROCAL EFFECT OF THEORY AND PRACTICE.

A particular difficulty in the nature of psycho-analysis itself makes the problem of the reciprocal effect of theory and practice even more complicated in this case than it is, perhaps, in other spheres of knowledge. The psycho-analytic technique was originally, and is still to-day, a means to a causal therapy of the neuroses and aims to allay symptoms by making their unconscious roots conscious. The therapy itself, therefore, seems to rest on a kind of "knowledge" which would thus itself be closely related to theoretic knowledge. But just psycho-analysis could for the first time clearly show that there are, so to speak, two kinds of knowledge, one intellectual, the other based on a deeper "conviction"; the clear cut distinction between these two, particularly in the sphere of psycho-analysis, must be considered among the first and strictest requirements.[21] This appears to be one of the reasons why psycho-analysis lays claim to a peculiar position, for here "plausibility" and "logical necessity" do not suffice as criteria of truth, but rather a direct perception or the experience of the problems in question is necessary in order to be convincing. This "experience," however, contains at the same time certain sources of error if one is not able, to a very great extent, in crystallizing the theoretic results out of the mental experience, to eliminate again the subjective factor of one's own impressions.

With the development of psycho-analysis the thera-

21 See also *Glaube, Unglaube und Ueberzeugung.* Ferenczi, Populäre Vorträge über Psychoanalyse.

peutic technique became increasingly more complete and detailed and this indeed with the help of this technique itself, which was thus at the same time a practical instrument for healing, as well as one of perception, since the patient was cured by his "knowledge." This fact, that the scientific instrument is at the same time the curative one, is one of the peculiarities of psycho-analysis, whereas other sciences use methods to increase their knowledge which, in relation to the object, must be designated as destructive (anatomy, vivisection, etc.).[22] Analysis has, therefore, from the very beginning two quite different aspects which constantly touch, intersect and cross one another, and the only question is from what angle one views it. If one sees the analytic technique as a means for finding out new psychological facts and connections, that is, for the investigation of mental life, one will be able to say that its therapeutic value is purely accidental; or, on the contrary, looked at from the standpoint of therapy, the scientific results would be a welcome by-product.

In "The Future Chances of Psycho-analytic Therapy"[23] Freud has already stated in anticipation the essentials of what can, in general, be said about the reciprocal relation between psycho-analytic technique and therapy. He says there, among other things, that the therapy will show much better, and probably quicker, results when we have more knowledge. Technical difficulties and the necessity for struggling with them were

[22] This difference seems to rest, according to Freud, on a peculiar and unique quality of mental life whereby the same psychic contents are given in various versions and can be topically separated from one another (see the topography in Freud's metapsychology). This makes it possible to make the patient live through the past mnemonically (and also in hallucination), and at the same time be the object of observations in the present without being obliged to "disturb" his present personality.

[23] Paper at the second Psycho-analytic Congress in Nürnberg, 1910.

the actual motives which led Freud to all those researches which resulted in the discovery of the unconscious mental life, its mechanisms, dynamics and economics, the knowledge of which then reapplied could increase our technical ability in the sense discussed above. One can here speak not of a vicious circle constantly creating new difficulties, but rather of a benign circle, of a mutual beneficial influence of the practice upon the theory and the theory upon the practice.

It is perhaps not an exaggeration to state that this kind of mutual control, of perception by experience (empiricism, induction) and in turn of experience by the preceding perception (systematization, deduction) is the only way of keeping a science from falling into error. A discipline which satisfies itself with one or the other methods of research alone, or too soon gives up the control offered by a counter experiment, would be doomed to sterility, pure empiricism because the productive thought would fail, pure theory because in premature omniscience the motives to further investigation would be silenced.

Freud's psycho-analysis deserves, in the theory of science, to be regarded as an example of correct "utraquistic"[24] research. It takes its roots in the necessity for favorably influencing certain mental functions which have fallen into the wrong grooves; i.e., it is based on reality. And psycho-analysis always turned back to this source if it wished to test the soundness of the theories which experience forced upon one, or logical necessity demanded. To illustrate the advantages of this interaction of theory and practice we would like here to point

[24] Utraquists were a religious sect who believed in partaking of both the bread and wine of communion; hence "utraquistic" or two sided.

to certain important stages of development in the Freudian investigations.

The first theory of Breuer and Freud, that of the abreaction of the strangulated affects, that the psyche possessed the ability to loosen affects from their original objects and to displace them upon others, apart from the fact that it made certain phenomena of mental life more plausible and comprehensible, rested entirely upon the therapeutic result of the cathartic probing into the memories in hysteria. Of course this knowledge then made the cathartic method itself, that is the search for the pathologic memories, very much easier.

The practical difficulty that one can hypnotize very few people correctly caused Freud to give up hypnosis, and then other methods of suggestion, and to allow his patients to associate freely. Thus one obtained surprising insight into unconscious material which had up to then been covered up by the hypnotic binding of the affect. The technique of free association led chiefly to the discovery of the content and forms of expression of unconscious thinking. The "fundamental rule" of the psycho-analytic technique of free association then produced the material which enabled Freud to establish the topical-dynamic point of view, later increased by the economic to the metapsychological attitude. Naturally, the theory then made an orientation in the material, obtained by free association, which could not be clearly understood, easier and set the practical task of understanding the individual case.

Since in every case of neurosis, without exception, sexual traumata in childhood had shown themselves to be the focus of the symptoms, one first set up the "traumatic theory" of hysteria. But, when it became evident that such traumata as could not possibly have occurred in reality, also came up for discussion in the free associations, Freud had to decide upon a modification of the theory which took into consideration the psychic as well as the outer reality, and particularly phantasies, as a factor in creating symptoms. What great progress this knowledge meant for analytic psychology, and how it advanced the practice and the technique of analysis need hardly be discussed here in detail.

The practical necessity, in certain cases of anxiety-hysteria, of forcing the patient, besides the free associations, to a certain overcoming of pain, as Freud described,[25] led to a consideration of all the work which the patient accomplished in the cure besides frank speaking. The theoretic observation of such mental phenomena, as occur as the result of "active" intervention, then gave us a deep insight into the dynamics of mental life in general, and we have in the course of our discussion, been able to point out to what an unexpected degree the use of "activity" in its broader sense furthers the practical work of the therapy.

The recent works of Freud, which attempt to construct the psychology of the Ego, which has up to now been neglected in favor of the study of the Libido, show plainly that our therapeutic and technical ability had also in this point gone very much ahead of our scientific knowledge. Particularly Freud's last work, the overture of which,— so to speak—we heard at the seventh congress in Berlin,[26] attempts to bring up to date and to harmonize some of the simple facts of experience, resulting from practice, with

[25] *Wege der psychoanalytischen Therapie.* Vortrag auf dem V Psychoanalytischen Kongress, Budapest, 1918.

[26] *Das Ich und das Es*—which has since appeared *in toto*.

our theoretic knowledge, or rather to enlarge and modify the latter insofar as it has proved insufficient for the explanation of these facts.

One could perhaps sum up the impression produced by these examples thus: Just as the first fundamental theoretic conceptions of Freud, worked out with exacting detail from countless impressions of experience, were the most effective stimulus to the development of the actual analytical technique—in contrast to the former method of practice,—so in increasing measure, as we have learned to understand and control the unconscious, a new piece of theory has been necessary which has again increased our technical ability.

Psycho-analysis seems now to have reached a point of development where our knowledge, of the previously neglected, but larger part of mental life, is sufficient to obtain important therapeutic results, *provided that one clearly understands how this knowledge can be effectively put into practice.* We have evidently taken this cardinal point much too little into account. It seems rather, that in the analyses, frequently that which was theoretically significant, rather than what was analytically important was sought for, whereas, on the other hand, what was practically important was often easily overestimated in the theory.

To put it extremely the problem could be formulated somewhat as follows: Psycho-analysis, which has developed from a therapy into a science, even into an attitude towards life, must carefully differentiate what part of this great theoretic structure has remained essential therapy, in the narrower sense of the word. Instead of mistakenly applying the theory "therapeutically" in a lump, one should rather ask oneself what part of the whole of psycho-analysis has proven suitable for application in medicine, and what remains as general psychological knowledge, as theory, or at the utmost as "therapy of the normal" (pedagogy). Thus, for example, the "complexes" are results of the theory which retain their value for normal psychology, their establishment must be a preliminary assumption and can never be the outcome of therapeutic endeavor (to analyze out a complex). It was a comprehensible, but fatal, mistake of some of our adherents to think that in the analysis the mere finding of the mistake in development should at once have a therapeutic effect; in contrast to this one-sided "socratic" interpretation the actual effective remedy must be sought in properly connecting the affects with the intellectual sphere.

Just as there are naturally and necessarily, advantageous mutual reactions between theory and practice, so necessarily the difference between the two resulted in disturbing and suppressing influences on both sides. We have already shown, in the critical chapter, what we chiefly mean by the disturbing influence of the theory on the practice. In general one may say that the advantages which accrued for normal psychology out of the magnificent increase of our knowledge of the unconscious were not always sufficiently used to further therapeutic interests. On the other hand, too much theoretic knowledge was often a hindrance to practical accomplishment. The analyst with too much knowledge has, so to speak, "the faults of his advantages." In a young science, in a state of development such as psycho-analysis was, one could find it justifiable that the analytic practitioner was able to combine the two tasks of healing and research, as Freud himself did in such an exemplary way. One can readily understand, however, that the attempt to follow this example frequently led more to a mixing up of these tasks than to their combination.

The theoretic analyst always runs the danger of looking, for example, for arguments to prove the correctness of a new statement, while he thinks that he is promoting the process of curing a neurosis. Important proofs for certain theories could be found in this way, but the process of healing the abnormal dynamics of mental life was scarcely promoted.

The first communications of Breuer and Freud, which still dealt exclusively with a few simple conceptions, told of splendid cures which were effected, sometimes in a few days or weeks. All of us have experinced similar good results, at the beginning of our psycho-analytic careers, some of us, perhaps, before we began to use analysis, for cures can be made with all psycho-therapeutic measures, but on account of the lack of knowledge of the processes used cannot be any evidence for or against the methods. To what extent this is true also of psycho-analysis, which, in fact, has never overestimated its therapeutic results, which are to-day unquestioned, we shall briefly discuss in our last chapter. When, with the increase of our knowledge on the whole, and with the experience of the individual analyst, such "wonder" cures became constantly more infrequent, and the analyses themselves longer, we should like to have these facts used as little against the psycho-analytic theory as in the beginning the quick results were used in favor of it. The cures, which one succeeded in making with less knowledge, are certainly not to be compared in value to those based on a deeper insight, even though these require more time. The length of the time required can never be an argument against the correctness of a method if only one can later prove that this prolongation was necessary and unavoidable in obtaining a better result, *i.e.,* a causal operating therapy.[27] One must recommend practitioners to fill out the gaps in their theoretic knowledge by necessary study, and analyses of themselves, and one should recommend those given to too much theory to push their academic interests aside as much as possible in their practical applications. This requiring as theoretically unbiased an attitude as possible must not be counted against us as an unscientific tendency. We fully appreciate the value for the promotion of science of the requisite scientific attitude which is connected with working with one's interests concentrated on a subject to be theoretically studied. Our criticism is directed against overestimating, or remaining fixed, in this or that phase of the development of psycho-analysis, particularly at those points at which the proper relation between theory and practice had not been sufficiently recognized, or taken into account, in that much which was correct only in a certain connection, and at a certain stage of our knowledge, was taken either too literally or too generally. We think, therefore, that most of the deficiencies in technique and certain consequent therapeutic difficulties are to be regarded as the results of an insufficient orientation as to the real nature of the psycho-analytic method and the actual meaning and goal of psycho-analytic treatment.

[27] The patients who complained of the length of the psychoanalytic treatment were in a certain sense right. We could, however, say to ourselves with a free conscience that this increase in the duration of the treatment meant a better result in the end.

CHAPTER V.

The beginnings of psycho-analysis were purely practical. Very soon, however, as a by-product of the therapeutic influencing of neurotics, there resulted a scientific insight into the construction and function of the mental apparatus, into the history of the individual and the species and, finally, into the biological foundations (the theory of the instincts).

The chief result of the favorable reaction of this knowledge on psycho-analytic practice was the discovery of the Oedipus complex as the nuclear complex of the neuroses, and the significance of the repetition of the Oedipus relation in the analytic situation (transference).

The essential thing in the analytical intervention, however, does not consist either in the verification of the "Oedipus Complex", or in the simple repetition of the Oedipus situation in the relation to the analyst, but rather in the setting free and detachment of the infantile libido from its fixation on its first objects.

Thus the psycho-analytic method of treatment, as we understand it to-day, developed into a method which has as its purpose the full re-living of the Oedipus situation in the relation of the patient to the analyst, in order to bring it, with the help of the patient's insight, to a new and more fortunate conclusion.

This relation develops of its own accord under the conditions of the analysis; the analyst then has the task of noticing its development from slight indications and of bringing the patient to a complete reproduction of the rela-

54

tion in the analytic experience. At times he must bring mere traces of the relationship to development by appropriate measures (activity).

The theoretic knowledge, in itself indispensable, of the development of the normal mental life, the theory of dreams, the sexual theory and so forth, must be used in practice, only insofar as they help to make possible the desired reproduction of the Oedipus relation in the analytic situation, or to make it easier. To lose oneself in the details of the history of the development of the individual, without continually reconstructing these connections, is not only practically incorrect and futile, but yields theoretically fewer reliable results than those which have been confirmed by practice in accordance with the above presentation.

The scientific importance of correctly practiced technique which has hitherto been neglected must be properly estimated. Theoretic results must be applied mechanically to the theory much less frequently than heretofore, but a constant correction of the theory should result from the new insight gained in practice.

Psycho-analysis, starting from a purely practical point of departure, under the impression of the first surprising insight, reached a phase of understanding. The cures so startling in the beginning became, with the rapidly increasing knowledge of the common mental mechanisms, comparatively less satisfactory so that one had to consider how to bring the therapeutic ability into harmony with the newly acquired knowledge, which had progressed so far ahead.

Our own presentation, described from this point of view, represents the beginning of a phase which we should like, in contrast to the previous ones, to call the phase of experience. Whereas formerly, one tried to obtain the therapeutic result as a reaction to the enlightenment of the patient, we now try to place the knowledge obtained by psychoanalysis directly in the service of our therapy, by directly provoking the corresponding personal experience on the basis of our insight, and explaining to the patient only this experience, which is naturally directly evident to him also.

The knowledge on the basis of which we are able to intervene at the right place, and in the requisite degree, consists essentially of the conviction of the universal importance of certain fundamental early experiences—as for example the Oedipus conflict,—the traumatic effect of which in the analysis, like a provocative treatment in medicine, is kindled again and, under the influence of living through the experience consciously for the first time, is brought to a useful ending.

This kind of therapy is related, in a certain sense, to a technique of education because—like education itself—it consists, on account of the affective relation to the teacher, far more in experience than in the factor of enlightenment. Here also, as in medicine, the tremendous progress from purely intuitive—and therefore often mistaken—intervention to the introduction of the conscious analytical experience based on knowledge, repeats itself.

CHAPTER VI.

Although we could scarcely, as we said in the beginning, succeed in giving a complete picture of the history of psycho-analysis, under the heading of the reciprocal effect of theory and practice, we think that we have nevertheless sketched the history of its development, in broad outlines, and consider that we are in a position to foretell its future paths of development.

The evolution, as we have frequently described, starting from Breuer's catharsis, led to the actual Freudian psycho-analysis which, simultaneously with its constantly increasing technical development, became a scientific theoretic system which was the foundation of an entirely new psychology. We showed how the misunderstanding of this double rôle of psycho-analysis, and the unavoidable one-sidedness could result, indeed, had to result, in sometimes this meaning, sometimes that, being overestimated at the expense of the other. The last extreme swing of the pendulum was the excessive interest in theorizing, which showed itself according to the general impression, at the Berlin Congress (September, 1922). In our critical exposition, in view of this, we tried to give the necessary balance, by more strongly emphasizing the practical aspects, in doing which one could hardly avoid, indeed it was perhaps even necessary at times, to fall into the other extreme.

This warning to ourselves must not, however, keep us from thinking out possible further developments in this direction, if only in general terms, so that by consistently following out these thoughts we may come somewhere near the truth, at least in certain points.

In his speech at the Budapest Congress (September, 1918) on "Wege der Psychoanalytischer Therapie" (The Ways of Psycho-analytic Therapy) Freud has already predicted the essentials as he sees them. One is only surprised that such important ideas have, in practice, not been given the attention due them from our point of view.[28] Finally, indeed, it began to look as though psycho-analysis, which preëminently serves a practical purpose, was to be over-flooded by a wave of theoretic speculation. This caused us to take these arguments of Freud as a point of departure in order to emphasize once more the practical point of view also in its therapeutic importance, which Freud himself never lost sight of.

Psycho-therapists before Breuer were extremely active, as is well known, but they were merely active, by which we mean that they lacked the insight into the mental mechanisms of the illness, as well as into their own behavior and its effect. In so far as they instinctively happened upon what was correct for the case in question, they obtained, and certainly do obtain, results. These sprang from the kind of activity (energetic or affectionate) which they for the time being preferred, operating somewhat beneficially upon the patient without any knowledge of the process. The important advance, represented by Freud's psycho-analysis over Breuer's catharsis, for the therapy in general was the insight into the fundamental importance of the transference. All other progress in analytic technique

28 The attempt to create polyclinic institutions is a commendable exception; their foundation goes back, as is well known, to this suggestion of Freud. See "Bericht uber die Berliner Psychoanalytische Poliklinik" (März, 1920, bis Juni, 1922). (Report on the Berlin Psychoanalytic Polyclinic) by Dr. M. Eitingon (Internat. Zeitschrf. VIII, 1922; also separately published by the International Psycho-Analytic Press).

since then can be regarded essentially as the consistent development, and utilization of this fundamental insight which was Freud's advance over Breuer. But the essential theoretic advances of Freud also resulted from this practical point of view—for example the recognition of the infantile Oedipus kernel in the transference situation. And greatly as psycho-analytic therapy has developed in breadth and depth since its beginnings, Freud has never departed in his technique from the fundamental conception that the affective factor of experience is the essential factor of the cure.

This, of course, required the rare faculty of constantly reapplying the increasing knowledge to advance the actual therapeutic task. Evidently the ability is not given to everyone of purposely keeping the theoretic interest apart from the practical necessities, and at the same time of being able to combine the two to such an extent as is beneficial to each. Thus we can understand the theoretical exaggerations in practice, against which our critical remarks were chiefly directed, whereas our descriptive considerations were intended to show, by way of suggestion, how the entire psychological knowledge won from analysis can, and must be used in practice, that is as a factor of analytic experience.

It would be a mistake to conclude from the above that we underestimate the theory or the knowledge in itself. Such is in no way the case. Only we believe that in this respect a change in the previous attitude is unavoidable. We were always of the opinion that the analyst, like the specialist in every other subject, can never know enough, but we deny the necessity of initiating the patient into our whole knowledge every time, or of discovering afresh in every single case the psychological and theoretical knowledge derived from analysis, and thus trying to acquire a conviction which one should have brought with one.

This standpoint leads to a remark in regard to the possibilities of learning psycho-analysis. There was no such possibility for a long time. Beginning analysts were entirely dependent upon the knowledge they could get out of books. This knowledge was therefore theoretic and they simply tried to apply it to the patient. If they wished to go further than this there remained nothing to do except, as is usual in other branches of medicine, to treat the patient at the same time as a subject of investigation. In consequence of the purely theoretic preparation, this re- such on the *anima vili* was directed chiefly towards the theory. From such experiences it gradually became clear that the only proper preparation must be the actual experience of an analysis. Therefore the training schools attached to the polyclinics have made the rule that every one who wishes to devote himself to analysis shall first be analyzed by an experienced analyst. But just as in the therapeutic analyses the mere imparting of academic knowledge belongs, as it were, to the pediatrics of this subject, we believe that the correct didactic analysis is one that does not in the least differ from the curative treatment. How, indeed, shall the future analyst learn the technique if he does not experience it just exactly as he is to apply it later? Moreover, it depends upon the results of the analysis whether in a given case it is a question of didactic or a therapeutic analysis, whether the intention and qualification for the profession of psycho-analysis remain firm after the treatment.

In view of certain experiences, one might be tempted to ask oneself, whether our therapeutic analyses have not up to now often been too "didactic", whereas the so-called didactic analyses taught less analysis than the theory, which should only have been acquired separately later on. We could formulate our standpoint in these questions somewhat thus: *too much knowledge on the part of the patient should be replaced by more knowledge on the part of the analyst.* The analyst should not impart the theoretic knowledge which "occurs" to him in connection with the association material of the patient; that is he should not express, as it were, his own parallel associations, but he should work over the whole material in himself and only impart that which the patient absolutely requires for the analytic experience, and its understanding.

By placing the accent on the knowledge and the action of the analyst the picture of the analytic treatment could, at least outwardly, in time in a certain sense more nearly approximate that of the usual methods of treatment in nonanalytic psycho-therapy, or in general medicine. The enormous difference consists in the fact that the analyst can, on the basis of properly combining his knowledge with the individual material which the patient offers, determine exactly the time, the kind and the degree of his intervention, whereas this is determined in all other kinds of psycho-therapy either by sheer force, or by "artificial" intuition.

In hypnosis, for example, the physician generally obtained merely temporary and not radical results, because its application covered over all the vital psychic motives. This was why Freud gave up hypnosis and used the method of free association which gave us our first insight into the play of mental forces. However, one must admit with Freud that hypnosis owes its undeniable successes to the complete elimination of the intellectual (ethical, esthetic, etc.) resistances. If one could, for example, combine the inestimable advantage of the technique of hypnosis with the advantage of the analytic ability to free the hypnotic affect situation, a tremendous advance in our therapeutic ability would be achieved.

Psycho-analysis has already shed enough light on this problem to enable us to recognize the Oedipus situation as the nucleus of the hypnotic affect relation. But it has not yet been able to give us the deepest understanding of what is really specific to the hypnotic state. When we have fully understood the nature of the hypnotic attachment to the physician, which has not yet been really cleared up by the recognition of the nature of the transference, it is possible that we may come to a point when the analyst can use hynosis as a part of his technique, without being obliged to fear that he may not be able in the end to loosen the affective umbilical cord which attaches the patient to him. This possibility of readmitting hypnosis, or other suggestive methods, into our analytic therapy would perhaps be the culmination of the simplification of the analytic technique, towards which, according to our interpretation, we should be and are actually tending. The final goal of psycho-analysis is to substitute, by means of the technique, affective factors of experience for intellectual processes. It is well known that this is just what is achieved in an extreme way in hypnosis, in which conscious material is called forth or eliminated according to need.

An elimination, particularly of the intellectual resistances, is being increasingly required since psycho-analysis has begun to penetrate more generally into society, and people bring this knowledge as a means of resistance into the cure. This fact was not the least among the motives which obliged us unintentionally to change our technique and must force us to adjust it to the increasing enlightenment of society as to the cause and nature of the neuroses.

According to Freud the spread of psycho-analytic knowledge will, in time, automatically bring about the disappearance of those forms of neuroses which we have known up to now.

We see here again two kinds of knowledge at work, one that helps the therapy, that can even, by prophylaxis, prevent the neuroses (the analytic education of children), the other which takes the form of a hindrance in the cure. This last difficulty is paralyzed by the fact that, for the present, at any rate, the knowledge of the analyst is still always a good deal in advance of and superior to general knowledge.

Thus the whole development of the technique of psycho-analysis tends, according to us, to become essentially simplified in the near future. It is possible that this will increase the appearance of a certain monotony and sticking to formula, but after all the correct practitioner was always a craftsman also and, perhaps, should essentially be so. The application of such formulæ to the individual material which here represent simply the residue of hard won knowledge, still remains the essential in psycho-analysis, thus offering sufficient opportunity to the specially gifted as well as for further research. The reduction of the method to more simple actual facts—which our increasing knowledge should also require—would in any case in time achieve, the not to be underestimated practical result, that on the one hand, it would be much easier for doctors (not only psycho-therapeutists) to acquire psycho-analytic knowledge, but on the other hand to shorten and simplify the treatment.

From this point of view of the practical application the splendid isolation which was indispensable to the creation and development of psycho-analysis need then no longer be strictly adhered to: indeed, we should not wonder, if the point were finally reached when other psycho-therapeutic methods which had proven themselves useful according to analytic understanding (as we tried to show, for example, in hypnosis) were legitimately combined with psycho-analysis. Freud himself had such future possibility of the mass application of psycho-analytic therapy in mind when he expressed the opinion that it was very probable that "the pure gold of analysis might be freely alloyed with the copper of direct suggestion and that the hypnotic means of influence might again find its place." [29]

Of course when psycho-analytic knowledge has penetrated into general medical thinking in the form of a better understanding of human nature, the result will be that all intervention will be based on a more accurate estimate of the mental factors also, and therefore will be more purposeful and effective. Already to-day farsighted general practitioners, gynecologists, and surgeons have attempted the application of psycho-analysis and, in so far as they were successful, were undeniably able to reach results which were surprising to other specialists. For us, of course, these results are not surprising, since we expect an essential advance in all branches of medicine from the definite analytic training of all doctors. One may even expect that psycho-analytic knowledge, that is the knowledge of mankind, may become the nucleus of all medical knowledge and bring about the unification of this science, which has been so dismembered by the extensive growth of the specialties. The old family physician, the friend and counselor of the family, would thus again play his former important rôle with an even deeper meaning. He would watch with understanding and know intimately the whole

[29] Wege der Psychoanalytischen Therapie, 1918.

personality and would be able to exert an intelligent influence upon the development of a human being from his birth onwards, on his education, to throw some light on the difficulties of puberty and the choice of a profession, and on marriage, all more or less trying mental conflicts, as well as to deal with organic illnesses and mental disorders. His rôle of counselor would not be restricted to bodily ailments, but he would give competent advice about the almost more important mental factors, such as the mutual influence of the mental and the physical.

This doctor of souls would naturally exert through the family a still unconceived amount of influence upon society, its morals and its customs, and thus indirectly effect an improvement in education, and in this way again contribute to the prophylaxis of the neuroses. The uniting, in the person of the physician, of knowledge which has up to now appeared to be so heterogeneous might possibly contribute towards the unification of the sciences in general, which up to now have been much too sharply separated into the natural and the mental sciences. We can already say that the penetration of psycho-analytic knowledge has, for example, greatly furthered the study of biology, by laying the foundation for an entirely new theory of the instincts which could then point out the way for a new theory of development. The results of reapplying psycho-analysis, for example, to physiological chemistry (inner secretions, etc.) in its modern trends can as yet scarcely be estimated; and the analysis of the neuroses finally strikes upon the chemistry of sex, the importance of which Freud laid down in principle in his "Three Contributions to the Theory of Sex." And the toxic etiology of the psychoses which had previously been considered only from the one point of view, might, in connection with the psycho-analyses of these illnesses, still lead to therapeutic surprises.

In the future, not only will psycho-analytic knowledge be the common property of all physicians, which will be as indispensable as to-day, for example, the knowledge of anatomy and physiology, but there will, of course, be specially trained therapeutists who, as is frequently the case to-day, need not necessarily be doctors since education as well as the care of mental life, are really psycho-therapeutic or prophylactic tasks. This settles the somewhat elaborate questioning of certain specialists as to whether "laymen", that is, nonmedical people, shall analyze at all. As the situation stands to-day physicians limited by their one-sided training in the natural sciences are actually laymen in psychological matters.[30] Indeed, one may truthfully say that their purely physiological way of thinking has, to a certain extent, limited their understanding of the mental side. On the other hand, the fundamental conceptions of psycho-analysis rest on a few general hypotheses common to human nature, so that aside from a thorough analytical training, a good general education suffices for its understanding and mastery and a knowledge of medicine is not necessarily advantageous as follows from what Freud says on this subject.[31] This was why the meaning of psychoanalysis was so much more recognized and appreciated up to now by nonmedical than by medical people, so much so that recently a young representative of modern psychiatry

[30] Only very recently has one thought of giving psychological training in medical schools.

[31] Ueber Psychoanalyse, 1910. ''The physician who through his training has come to know so much which is a closed chapter to the layman, is helpless before hysterical phenomena in spite of his knowledge.'' ''He himself is a layman in the face of hysteria; he cannot understand it.'' Therefore, Freud also says that it is only advantageous to us to go with the physician up to the point of diagnosis, but that we can then separate from him.

could in an open meeting of a congress reproach his colleagues with the fact that they, who really were called upon to be the leaders in psycho-analysis, had let the subject slip out of their hands.[32] This state of affairs should, however, improve in the near future and it looks as though in certain countries official medicine were beginning to take a different stand, so that the looked-for penetration of psycho-analysis into the general knowledge of mankind will bring about the disappearance of disputes about borderline cases among specialists.

What Freud was already able to foretell in "The Future Chances of Psycho-analytic Therapy" (in his Congress speech, 1910), that our therapeutic results will be much better when we shall have obtained the authority commonly attributed to other specialists, has since then come to pass to some extent. However, the full effectiveness of these social factors, which must in no way be underestimated, will only be achieved when the resistances—intellectual and others—will have disintegrated, perhaps with the assistance of changes in the technique which take these points into account.

If we have attempted in the foregoing pages, venturing from the present direct facts, to forecast the prospects of psycho-analysis, this seems to us more than an idle play of phantasy. Indeed, if we carry these thoughts to their logical conclusion, we come to a point at which our interpretation appears in so far to be justified as it fits in with that of a great, if indirect, organic development. / The most important advance in psycho-analysis consists finally in a great increase of consciousness, or expressed according to our meta-psychology, in raising the instinctive unconscious mental content to the level of pre-conscious thinking. This,

[32] See Prinzhorn's Review of (his own work) Inter-n. Zeitschrift f. PsA. VIII, 1922.

however, from our point of view, means such an important step in the development of mankind, that it may actually be regarded as a biologic advance, and indeed as one which for the first time takes place under a kind of self-control.

Under the influence of this increase in consciousness the physician, who has developed from the medicine man, sorcerer, charlatan, and magic healer, and who at his best often remains somewhat an artist, will develop increasing knowledge of mental mechanisms, and in this sense, prove the saying that medicine is the oldest art and the youngest science.